AF428401

Our
Rainbow
Road

WRITTEN BY TORI FLETES
ILLUSTRATED BY WOAO

For years and years I dreamed of you
Did all the things that I could do

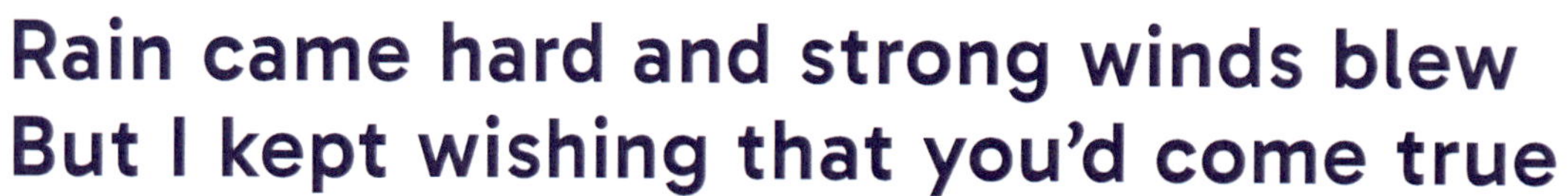

Rain came hard and strong winds blew
But I kept wishing that you'd come true

The sun came up and what do you know?
I looked out the window and saw a rainbow

In my hands I held 10 little toes
Saw 10 little fingers and a button nose

I worked hard for you, I promise this
There's not one day you won't be kissed
I cried for you and would not quit
Reminded myself I had to persist

But all good things are worth the fight
You're no exception, you're the sunlight

Even with nothing but rain in the sky
There's surely a rainbow to stop by

Always try to do the best you can
Be anything you want, be strong like dad

Be a doctor, a pilot, or have a rock band
Be silly, be serious, or a big smarty pants

You'll do great things, you already have
You stuck around when others passed

HA!
HA! HA!

You made a rainbow that was here to last
Got rid of my tears when I needed a laugh

So let's ride down our own rainbow road
I'll go wherever you want to go
Over the red and to the yellow
Wild as a Dino or chill as a toad

I love you more than I can say
I'll love you each and every day

I'm thankful you are here to stay
You are my rainbow, for you I prayed

"Created with love for our favorite people in the world."